RUCKER SCHOOL
GUSD
GILROY, CA 95020

S0-AWG-115

Leatherback Sea Turtle

Rod Theodorou

Heinemann Library
Chicago, Illinois

© 2001 Reed Educational & Professional Publishing
Published by Heinemann Library,
an imprint of Reed Educational & Professional Publishing,
Chicago, IL

Customer Service 888-454-2279

Visit our website at www.heinemannlibrary.com

All rights reserved. No part of this publication may be reproduced or transmitted in any form or by any means, electronic or mechanical, including photocopying, recording, taping, or any information storage and retrieval system, without permission in writing from the publisher.

Designed by Ron Kamen

Illustrations by Dewi Morris/Robert Sydenham

Originated by Ambassador Litho Ltd.

Printed and bound in Hong Kong/China

05 04 03 02 01
10 9 8 7 6 5 4 3 2 1

Library of Congress Cataloging-in-Publication Data
Theodorou, Rod.
  Leatherback sea turtle / Rod Theodorou.
    p. cm. -- (Animals in danger)
  Includes bibliographical references and index (p.).
  ISBN 1-57572-272-0 (library)
  1. Leatherback turtle--Juvenile literature. 2. Endangered species--Juvenile literature. [1. Leatherback turtle. 2. Turtles. 3. Endangered species.] I. Title.

QL666.C546 T44 2001
597.92'89--dc21   00-063265

Acknowledgments
The author and publishers are grateful to the following for permission to reproduce copyright material: Ardea, p. 12; Ardea/Francois Gohier, p. 4; Ardea/Masahiro Lijima, pp. 16, 26; Bat Conservation International/Merlin D. Tuttle, p. 4; BBC/Lynn M. Stone, p. 4; Bruce Coleman/Gerald S. Cubitt, p. 20; FLPA/Fritz Polking, p. 22; NHPA/Anthony Bannister, p. 14; NHPA/Peter Pickford, p. 8, NHPA/Jany Sauvanet, p. 18; OSF, p. 13; OSF/David Cayless, p. 24; OSF/Olivier Grunewald, pp. 9, 15, 19, 21; OSF/John Mitchell, p. 27; Doug Perrine/Seapics, pp. 6, 7, 11; Still Pictures, p. 5, Still Pictures/Pascal Kobeh, p. 25; WWF Photolibrary, p. 17; WWF Photolibrary/Alain Compost, p. 23.

Cover photograph reproduced with permission of Bruce Coleman/Gerald S. Cubitt.

Every effort has been made to contact copyright holders of any material reproduced in this book. Any omissions will be rectified in subsequent printings if notice is given to the publisher.

Some words are shown in bold, **like this.** You can find out what they mean by looking in the glossary.

Contents

Animals in Danger

whooping crane

gray bat

polar bear

All over the world, more than 25,000 animal **species** are in danger. Some are in danger because their homes are being destroyed. Many are in danger because people hunt them.

4

This book is about leatherback sea turtles and why they are **endangered**. Unless people protect them, leatherback sea turtles will become **extinct**. We will only be able to find out about them from books like this.

What Are Leatherback Sea Turtles?

Leatherback turtles are **reptiles**. They are the largest **marine** turtles in the world. They travel farther and dive deeper than any other turtle.

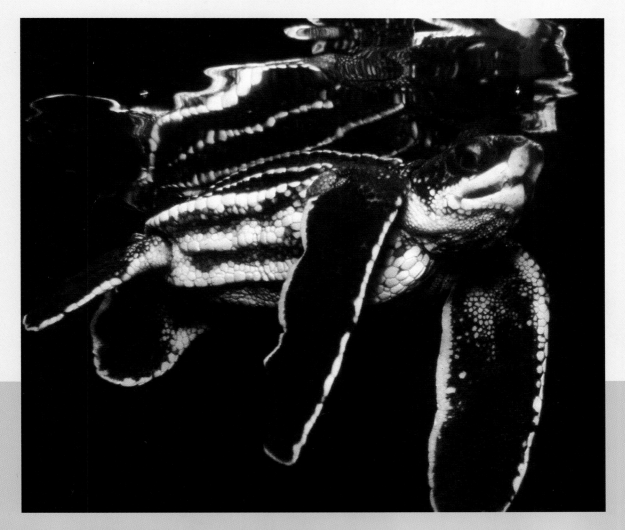

Marine turtles spend their whole lives in the ocean. They have to come to the surface to breathe air. All marine turtles are **endangered** animals.

What Do Leatherback Sea Turtles Look Like?

Leatherback sea turtles have very large front flippers. This makes them strong swimmers. They have seven long ridges running down their shells.

Leatherbacks are named after their shells. All other turtles have hard shells. Leatherbacks have rubbery shells that feel like wet **leather**.

Where Do Leatherback Sea Turtles Live?

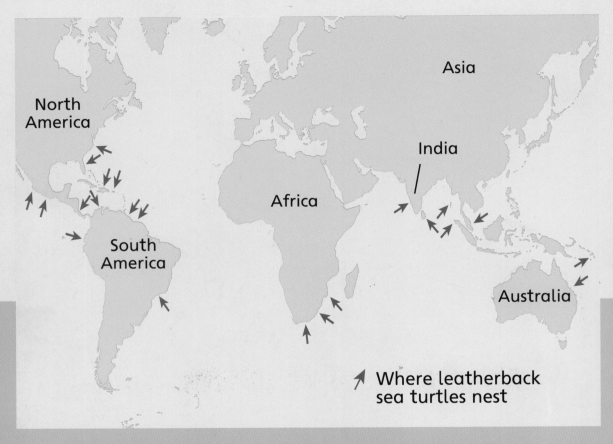

Where leatherback sea turtles nest

Leatherbacks swim in all the warm waters of the world. They nest on the beaches of North America, South America, India, and parts of Africa and Asia.

Leatherbacks are such strong swimmers that they can swim in the open ocean, a long way from land. All other **marine** turtles always swim close to the coasts.

What Do Leatherback Sea Turtles Eat?

Leatherback turtles are **omnivores**. Their favorite food is **jellyfish**. They will also eat seaweed, **mollusks,** and small fish.

Leatherbacks can eat twice their weight in jellyfish every day! The jellyfish stings do not hurt them or make them sick.

Leatherback Sea Turtle Babies

In spring, at night, **female** leatherbacks swim up to a sandy beach. They pull themselves out of the water and crawl up the beach. Then they dig a hole with their back flippers.

14

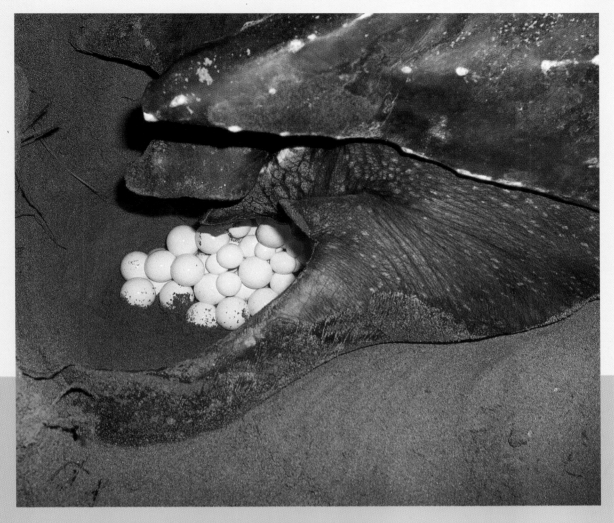

The females lay about 60 white eggs in the nest. They cover up the eggs with sand. Then they return to the ocean.

Race for the Sea

About two months later the eggs hatch. The tiny baby leatherbacks dig themselves out of the sand and crawl toward the ocean.

Sea birds, crabs, and other animals attack the baby turtles. In the water, sharks and other big fish eat them. Many die, but many others escape and swim away.

Unusual Leatherback Sea Turtle Facts

After a **female** turtle has laid her eggs, she returns to the ocean. It may be two or three years before she goes to land again to lay more eggs. **Males** spend their entire lives in the ocean.

Female leatherbacks can swim more than 2,500 miles from the beach where they laid their eggs. When it is time to lay more eggs they find their way back to exactly the same beach.

How Many Leatherback Sea Turtles Are There?

It is very hard to count leatherbacks in the oceans, but we can count their nests. In 1992, a nest count showed there were about 70,000 **female** leatherbacks.

We know there are fewer leatherback nests each year. Many beaches have no nests at all. Now there may be only 39,000 female leatherback sea turtles left.

Why Is the Leatherback Sea Turtle in Danger?

Leatherbacks like soft, sandy beaches to nest on. These are also the beaches that people like. This is bad news for the turtles.

Beach chairs, boats, and bright lights confuse and frighten the **female** turtles. People also steal their eggs and hunt the grown-up turtles for food.

Many turtles are caught in nets that have been put out to **trawl** for **shrimp.** About 1,500 turtles die every year in shrimp nets.

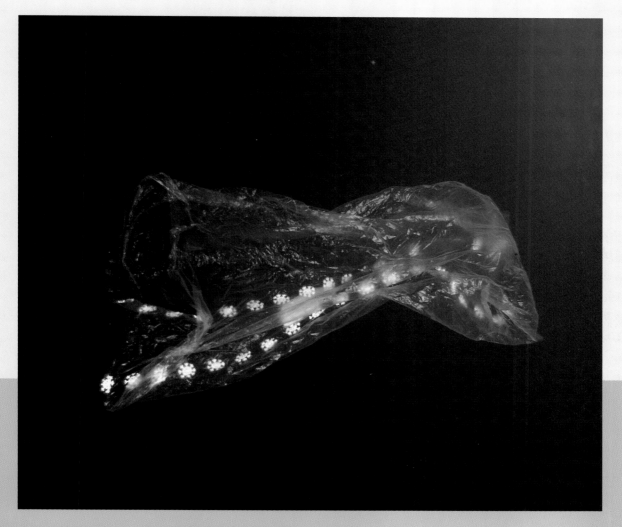

Sometimes leatherback turtles eat poisonous balls of **tar** from oil spills. People's trash ends up in the ocean. Floating plastic bags and balloons look like **jellyfish.** If the turtles eat them, they can die.

How Is the Leatherback Sea Turtle Being Helped?

Stealing turtle eggs is now **illegal** in most countries. Scientists and police **patrol** the beaches at night, but it is hard to protect all the nests from egg thieves.

Sometimes scientists dig up the eggs and take them to a safe place to hatch. The turtles grow bigger. Then the scientists take them back to the beach. They let the turtles go at night, when it is safer.

Leatherback Sea Turtle Fact File

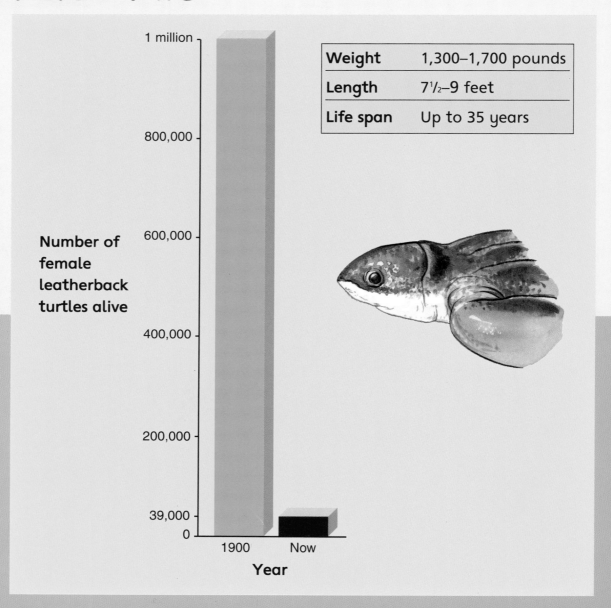

Weight	1,300–1,700 pounds
Length	7½–9 feet
Life span	Up to 35 years

Number of female leatherback turtles alive

1 million

800,000

600,000

400,000

200,000

39,000

0

1900   Now

Year

World Danger Table

	Number when animal was listed as endangered	Number that may be alive today
Leatherback Sea Turtle	135,000	15,000
American Crocodile	1,000–2,000	500–1,000
Galapagos Tortoise	250,000	15,000
Komodo Dragon	unknown	3,000–5,000
Loggerhead Sea Turtle	about 70,000 females	60,000 females

There are thousands of other reptiles in the world that are in danger of becoming **extinct**. This table shows some of these animals.

Can you find out more about them?

How Can You Help the Leatherback Sea Turtle?

If you and your friends raise money for the leatherback sea turtle, you can send it to these organizations. They take the money and use it to pay **conservation** workers and to buy food and tools to help save the leatherback sea turtle.

Defenders of Wildlife
1101 Fourteenth St., N.W. #1400
Washington, DC 20005

World Wildlife Fund
1250 Twenty-fourth St.
P.O. Box 97180
Washington, DC 20037

More Books to Read

Arnold, Caroline. *Sea Turtles.* New York: Scholastic, Inc., 1994.

Johnston, Marianne. *Sea Turtles: Past and Present.* Minneapolis, Minn.: Lerner Publishing Group, Inc., 1998. An older reader can help you with this book.

Stone, Lynn M. *Sea Turtles.* Vero Beach, Fla.: Rourke Publishing, 1993

Glossary

endangered   group of animals that is dying out, so there are few left

extinct   group of animals that has completely died out and can never live again

female   girl or woman

illegal   against the law

jellyfish   animals that live in the ocean and have bodies that are soft like jelly

leather   type of tough material made from the skin of animals

male   boy or man

marine   something that lives in the ocean

mollusk   animal with a shell covering its body, like a snail

omnivore   animal that eats both plants and animals

patrol   to guard an area

reptiles   snakes, lizards, crocodiles, turtles, tortoises and other animals that are cold-blooded and covered in scales

shrimp   small sea animal that has many legs and a shell around its body

species   group of animals that are very similar

tar   sticky chemical made from oil

trawl   to catch fish or other seafood with a large net that is dragged along the bottom of the ocean

Index